J. I. PACKER

KNOWING

GOD

STUDY GUIDE

*Fiftieth
Anniversary
Edition*

T0002164

An imprint of InterVarsity Press
Downers Grove, Illinois

InterVarsity Press
P.O. Box 1400 | Downers Grove, IL 60515-1426
ivpress.com | email@ivpress.com

InterVarsity Press® is the publishing division of InterVarsity Christian Fellowship/USA®. For more information, visit intervarsity.org.

While any stories in this book are true, some names and identifying information may have been changed to protect the privacy of individuals.

The publisher cannot verify the accuracy or functionality of website URLs used in this book beyond the date of publication.

Cover design: David Fassett
Interior design: Daniel van Loon
Cover images: Getty Images: © Peter Zelei Images, © Jackyenjoyphotography, © MirageC, © sergio34, © YOTUYA, © ulimi
ISBN 978-1-5140-0780-8 (print)
Printed in the United States of America ♾

31 30 29 28 27 26 25 24 23 | 13 12 11 10 9 8 7 6 5 4 3 2 1

CONTENTS

PREFACE

1975

I wrote *Knowing God* over a period of years during which I was deeply concerned, as I still am, to help people realize God's *greatness*. My own spiritual pilgrimage, such as it is, has been marked (thank God) by dawning light on this point. Before my conversion I was self-absorbed in just about every way, a silly, twisted adolescent who needed a great deal of straightening out. One milestone in this merciful process, so far as it has gone (and I do not suppose it has gone very far yet), has been the discovery that the first thing to ask of any Scripture is not what it tells me about myself, but what it says about my God. That is the open secret of right-minded and (to borrow a Puritan word) "soul-fatting" Bible study, and there is really no excuse for missing it. But I started off in Bible study on the wrong foot, and it took me years to get this lesson clear.

A second milestone has been the Copernican revolution in my outlook through realizing that I am not the center of things, but God is, and that I as his creature and child exist for him rather than he for me. This, too, was something which irreligious instincts continuing after conversion hid from me at the start. But the writings of four great God-centered men, John Charles Ryle, John Owen, John Calvin and Jonathan Edwards, helped me get it clear intellectually, and in coping with rough stuff from people whom I have loved and trusted I have found what strength and support come from learning, however incompletely, to put God first.

"Thus the Lord showed me," and *Knowing God* reflects it, and in that sense has in it more of me than anything else I have written; and the task of trying to tell people who God is remains a major part of what I take to be my ministry. So it has naturally meant much to me to learn how *Knowing God* has circled the globe and, as it seems, brought blessing wherever it has gone. I hope the use of this excellent study guide which the publishers have prepared may increase its ministry yet further.

It was suggested that, as part of this preface, I should mention any ideas which I now wish I had put in the book but did not, and any which I wish were not there but are. I can thankfully say that in *Knowing God*, as in my earlier writings, I find nothing I wish to withdraw. In fact, I get help from rereading it, as Richard Baxter did from rereading his books three centuries ago.

Nor do I find any omissions in terms of the overall plan. On God's *sovereignty*, I deliberately chose to write no separate chapter, but to deal with it as John Newton said he dealt with his Calvinism: He did not make an issue of it, but mixed it into his treatment of everything else, so that, like sugar in coffee, "it sweetens the whole." I followed the same policy with God's *holiness*, "the attribute of attributes," except that here the appropriate image would not be sugar so much as mustard. The lack of distinct presentations of these two basic aspects of God is thus formal rather than substantial. My categorizing of God's attributes has been criticized as old-fashioned, but I would rather have a scheme that is old-fashioned and clear than one that is modern and muddled. And I wrote for readers who would feel the same.

But one defect I do see. In addressing my readers as individuals, trying as best I can to single them out and search their hearts before God, I fail to show that it is only as one gives oneself in human relationships, in the home, in friendships, with neighbors, as members of Christian groups and teams—in relationships that go sometimes right and sometimes wrong, as all our relationships do—that experiential knowledge of God becomes real and deep. For ordinary people, to be a hermit is *not* the way! The buttoned-up Christian "loner" who keeps aloof and reads books like this (or just the Bible!) may pick up true notions of God as well as anyone else may, but only the Christian sharer, who risks being hurt in order to take and give the maximum in fellowship and who sometimes does get hurt as a result, ever knows much of God himself in experiential terms. This perspective, so clear in the Psalms (to which, perhaps, my book should be seen as a preamble, or maybe a footnote), is so vital that I am very much at fault for not having made more of it. But if *groups* use this study guide, as is intended, that in itself may yet induce the necessary open and mutually committed lifestyle which I failed to mark out in the exposition. I hope and pray so, anyway.

J. I. P.

INTRODUCTION

J. I. Packer's *Knowing God* is a rich, profound, delightful and transforming discussion of the Christian understanding of God. Written with great intensity yet superb control, it explains both who God is and how a human being can relate to him. The book has three sections: The first directs our attention to the hows and whys of knowing God, the second to the attributes of God, the third to some primary benefits enjoyed by a person who is God's child. Packer has produced a book likely to nurture generations of believers.

The author says that he wrote *Knowing God* from the conviction that ignorance of God lies at the root of the contemporary church's weakness. The purpose of this guide is to help the "sick tree" of Christendom ingest a vitamin-rich diet; or, to drop the metaphor, to help groups of Christians identify and apply the essential truths of biblical theology.

This guide contains twenty-two studies, one for each chapter of *Knowing God*. A gathering of Christians can use it to examine the entire book or to lead them into various chapters according to their purposes, interests and time limitations. A Sunday-school class or campus small group will find here two excellent eleven-week projects: (1) a survey of the attributes of

God (studies 7–17) and (2) an investigation of the privileges and problems of living as a Christian (studies 1–6, 18–22).

The structure of each study is this: First, a purpose sentence (or sentences) states the aim. It helps the participants know where they are going. Then follows the body of the discussion—a series of questions which move efficiently through all the material. Finally, a summary question helps to draw out the essence of the chapter.

Each session will take from thirty to sixty minutes, depending on how talkative the group members are. Each summary question is open-ended enough to be pursued at some length if the study is threatening to take less than the time you have. Furthermore, the shorter studies include an optional question which encourages the members to pick up an important point and develop it in detail.

Scattered throughout each study are two or three application questions. Each is designed to prompt personal sharing and an individualized response to the principles Packer sets forth. Answering an application question will take a minimum of five minutes (and should be held to a maximum of ten), so the application questions alone are likely to use up fifteen to thirty minutes and comprise from a quarter to a half of each discussion.

FOR THE LEADER

The questions provided here make up the skeleton of each study. They help you keep your group working steadily through the entire chapter, touching on all the main points and applying them appropriately. It is expected, though, that you will flesh out the discussion by using follow-up questions. For example, you may ask, "How does the love of God make a difference in your life day by day?" (a question from study 12), and someone may answer, "It helps me get through my work." Pursue that by asking further, "How does it do that?" or "What particular problems does it help you solve?" Also, summarize frequently to remind people where they have been and where they are going.

Do everything you can to encourage balanced discussion. When someone who talks a lot finishes a statement, invite further comment by saying something like, "Does anyone want to add to that?" or "Does someone have another idea?" Doing this will encourage quieter people to make contributions. But don't be afraid of silences in discussion. If the group is working together, silences can be periods of creative effort. If a silence goes too long, rephrase your question or try injecting some humor. If someone is continually dominating or silent, talk with that person privately to encourage more balanced participation. (You will find other helpful principles for leading in *Leading Bible Discussions* [IVP], especially in chapter eight.)

You may want to develop a regular habit of corporate worship in conjunction with each topic, raising up prayers of praise and thanksgiving or singing a hymn. Occasionally a time of talking to God is suggested as an optional activity when it is particularly appropriate. But let this be a stimulus to further worship, not a limit. (Rosalind Rinker's *Prayer: Conversing with God* and John Paterson's *How to Pray Together* are valuable resources in this area.)

Regarding preparation: Tell the members to read the chapter prior to the session. Encourage them to underline significant passages and ponder them and to come with reflections and queries to help move the discussion along. For your own part, take time (you'll probably need between two and three hours) to make the study your own. Write a brief answer to each question; then go back and, wherever necessary, put the questions into words and phrases you feel comfortable using. Make sure, however, that you don't stray from a question's intent.

Think about how this particular study relates to your friends' needs. Does John need to know that God really loves him? Does Dawn have an accurate concept of God's wrath? Lives change, so the application questions provided in this guide had to be general enough to fit a variety of life situations. Be sure you make them touch the lives of the people in your group.

Be sensitive to needs that emerge during the discussion, and be prepared to carry on a ministry between the sessions. Sit down and talk with people individually. Show your concern for the members in other practical ways.

Make sure everyone knows what to read for the first study, and then begin your own preparation—prayerfully eager to lead brothers and sisters in Christ into the adventure of knowing God.

THE STUDY OF GOD

PURPOSE:
To see why the study of God is important.

DISCUSSION:

1. For whom is Packer writing (pp. 11-12)? What does he mean by *traveler?*

2. What conviction lies behind the book (p. 12)?

3. In what ways does "contemplation of the Divinity" affect us?

4. What comes to your mind when you hear the word *theology?* What is your attitude toward theology? Why does Packer think that "a study of the nature and character of God . . . is the most practical project anyone can engage in"?

5. What attitude does Packer say we should assume when someone tells us "there is no road to knowledge about God"?

6. On page 20, Packer lists five basic truths by which we will plot our course in these studies. Read them aloud. What main themes will occupy us as we journey? How comfortable do you feel with these themes?

7. What should be our ultimate aim in studying the Godhead? Why does theological knowledge "go bad on us" if sought for its own sake?

8. Why did the writer of Psalm 119 want a knowledge of God? How does the "Knowledge Applied" section of this chapter (pp. 21-23) speak to *your* motives for undertaking this study?

9. How can we turn our knowledge *about* God into knowledge *of* God? What does it mean to *meditate?* How do you personally respond to Packer's description of meditation?

SUMMARY:
Why is the study of God important? How will knowing this affect your life this week?

THE PEOPLE WHO KNOW THEIR GOD

PURPOSE:
To consider whether we are people who know God.

DISCUSSION:

1. On pages 24-25, what charge does Packer level against evangelicals? How true is this of you?

2. Packer says, "One can know a great deal about God without much knowledge of him." What does this sentence mean?

3. What does this sentence mean: "One can know a great deal about godliness without much knowledge of God"?

4. What are four characteristics of people who do know God?

5. What is it that goads God's people into action? Why is "the invariable fruit of true knowledge of God . . . energy to pray" (p. 29)?

6. What is the central truth about God taught in the book of Daniel?

7. Why are our prayers the best evidence of our view of God? Think back over your prayers of the past day or week. What view of God did they imply?

8. How would you describe the spirit of Daniel and his three friends? What produced it?

9. Why is knowing God the basis of genuine personal peace?

10. Packer suggests that if we desire to know God we should do two things. What are they? How do you think we can do them day by day?

SUMMARY:
Packer says that each of the four characteristics listed on pages 27-31 is a "sign" or "test" of a person's knowledge of God. Where are you strongest? weakest?

KNOWING AND BEING KNOWN

PURPOSE:
To understand what it means to know God.

DISCUSSION:

1. Read aloud the first five paragraphs on page 33. What should be our purpose in life?

2. Consider the next three sentences (pp. 33-34). What impact did the first five paragraphs have on *you?* What, then, may this indicate about your stance before God?

3. Why are Christians immune from Absurdist tapeworms and Antoinette's fever?

4. What does it mean to *know* someone?

5. On pages 35-36, how does Packer illustrate our relationship with God? Do you think it is a good analogy? Why or why not?

6. What happens when the Almighty Creator, "before whom the nations are as a drop in a bucket," breaks through to an individual and speaks to him personally? Are you thrilled at being God's covenant partner?

7. What four things does the activity of knowing God involve?

8. What four analogies does the Bible use to describe our relationship with God? What do they have in common?

9. How is a contemporary Christian's relationship with Jesus different from the relationship Jesus' first disciples had with him? How is it the same?

10. What does it mean to say that knowing God is a matter "of personal dealing"? "of personal involvement"? "of grace"?

11. Why is the fact that God knows us more important than the fact that we know God?

SUMMARY:
What does it mean to know God?

THE ONLY TRUE GOD

PURPOSE:
To understand the meaning of idolatry and how idolatry affects our knowledge of God.

DISCUSSION:

1. To what principle does the second commandment point us? On page 44, how does Packer apply this principle to Christians?

2. How do images dishonor God?

3. How do images mislead people?

4. Packer says, "Psychologically, it is certain that if you habitually focus your thoughts on an image or picture of the One to whom you are going to pray, you will come to think of him, and pray to him, as the image represents him." Have you been trained or encouraged to focus on some image of God? What steps can you take to free your mind from images?

5. Why is a false mental image as harmful to knowing God as a physical representation?

6. What is the positive purpose of the second commandment?

7. What does Packer say is the relationship between focusing on images and heeding God's Word? How does the Jews' experience on Sinai support this contention?

8. Packer summarizes: "All manmade images of God, whether molten or mental, are really borrowings from the stock-in-trade of a sinful and ungodly world, and are bound therefore to be out of accord with God's own holy Word." Do you agree? If so, what in Packer's argument convinces you? If not, explain why.

9. What test does Packer give for determining whether your God is the Christian God? How do your ideas about God measure up to this test?

   Optional: What implications does Packer's argument in the first part of this chapter have for Christian art? For instance, how would his view affect an artist's choice of subject?

SUMMARY:
How can images keep us from knowing God?

GOD INCARNATE

PURPOSE:

To consider the mystery of the Incarnation.

DISCUSSION:

1. What is "the supreme mystery with which the gospel confronts us"?

2. Give specific illustrations of how believing in the Incarnation dissolves other difficulties in Christian doctrine.

3. *The baby born at Bethlehem was God.* How does the apostle John structure the prologue to his Gospel to make clear what the title *Son of God* means? What seven things does he tell us about the Word who became flesh?

4. *The baby born at Bethlehem was man.* On page 57, how does Packer describe the "mathematics" of the Incarnation? How did the Incarnation change Jesus' relation to the devil?

5. Why should the Incarnation move us to praise God for his humility?

6. What was the *motive* for the Incarnation?

7. What is the *kenosis theory*? What are some of the ways in which it has been formulated? Why will this theory not stand?

8. What does this statement mean: "The impression . . . is not so much one of deity reduced as of divine capacities restrained"? How can we account for this restraint?

9. What, in your own words, is "the Christmas spirit"? How is the church today failing to exhibit it? What are some specific actions you could perform to manifest the Christmas spirit?

SUMMARY:

Why is the Incarnation the supreme mystery of the gospel? What effects should being aware of the Incarnation have on each of us?

HE SHALL TESTIFY

PURPOSE:

To understand the nature and importance of the work of the Holy Spirit.

DISCUSSION:

1. Do you feel the doctrine of the Trinity is as neglected as Packer says it is? How does the doctrine of the Trinity make a difference in your own life?

2. How does the Gospel of John teach us about the Trinity?

3. What are other translations of the term *Comforter*? What ideas does this word convey?

4. What is the relationship between the Spirit's work and Christ's work?

5. What does the Old Testament have to say about God's *Word* and God's *Spirit*?

6. On pages 67-68, Packer untangles the relations in the Trinity. What conclusions does he reach? What is his evidence for them?

7. Packer maintains that the church consistently ignores the work of the Holy Spirit. Do you agree? How does your awareness of the Spirit's work make a difference in your own life?

8. Why without the Holy Spirit would there be no gospel and no New Testament?

9. Why without the Spirit would there be no Christians?

10. In the section called "Our Proper Response," what is implied about how we can honor the Spirit in our faith? in our life? in our witness?

    Optional: Read Romans 8:1-30. Discuss the relationship a Christian should have to the Holy Spirit.

SUMMARY:

What is the work of the Holy Spirit? Why is it important?

GOD UNCHANGING

PURPOSE:

To grasp the fact and significance of God's immutability.

DISCUSSION:

1. What problem does Packer describe on page 75? To what extent do you identify with this problem?

2. Answer Packer's question: "How can this sense of remoteness from the biblical experience of God be overcome?"

3. State six aspects of God which do not change.

4. Contrast the *life* of God with the life of his creatures.

5. Contrast the stability of the Creator's *character* with that of men and women.

6. How do the two disclosures of God's name in Exodus supplement each other?

7. Contrast the *words* of God and the words of men and women.

8. What are some things God *does* today which he also did in Bible times? (For each item you list:) Why does he do it?

9. Why does God never need to repent? How does Packer explain the verses which speak of God's repenting? What effect should our awareness of "the immutability of God's decrees" have on us?

10. Why can Packer say that Jesus Christ's being "the same yesterday, and today, and forever" is "the strong consolation of all God's people"?

11. On what grounds is the sense of distance between us and believers in Bible times removed? What realities are the same for us as for them? How should this thought comfort us? challenge us?

    Optional: Read each of these verses aloud: Psalm 93:2; Jeremiah 10:10; Romans 1:22-23; 1 Timothy 6:16; Psalm 90:2; Psalm 102:26-27; Isaiah 48:12. What main impression do you get from hearing them read together?

SUMMARY:

What does it mean to say that God is *immutable*? Why is this important to you?

THE MAJESTY OF GOD

PURPOSE:

To appreciate the majesty of God.

DISCUSSION:

1. How does the Bible use the word *majesty*? How does this contrast with modern thoughts of God?

2. When we stress that God is personal, what must we be sure we do not communicate?

3. What "twin truths" about God are impressed upon us in the opening chapters of Genesis? Through what events is each one emphasized?

4. What two steps must we take to form a right idea of God's greatness?

5. On pages 85-86, Packer discusses Psalm 139 as an example of what the first step involves. How does this psalm highlight God's presence? his knowledge? his power?

6. In Isaiah 40, to what powerful forces is God compared? What is the nature of these comparisons? How do these comparisons affect you personally?

7. What three questions does Isaiah ask to the downcast Israelites? What does each question rebuke? What can we do to be guiltless of each rebuke?

   Optional: Read dramatically Job 38—41. How does God reveal his majesty? What effect does this have on Job (42:1-6)?

SUMMARY:

What have you learned about the majesty of God? How should this affect your worship? your moral decisions? your prayer life?

——∽∾∿——

GOD ONLY WISE

PURPOSE:

To appreciate and find comfort in God's wisdom.

DISCUSSION:

1. What is wisdom?

2. Why is God "utterly worthy of our fullest trust"?

3. What do many people mistakenly take to be God's goal in the world?

4. What *is* God's ultimate goal?

5. What are his immediate goals?

6. Why is the Lord Jesus central in the fulfillment of each part of God's purpose?

   Packer discusses God's wisdom in dealing with three men: Abraham, Jacob and Joseph.

7. What was Abraham like when God began to work with him? What was his greatest need? What were the characteristics of Abraham "the man of God"?

8. In what ways did Jacob need to be changed? How did God change him?

9. For what "double purpose" did Joseph suffer?

10. What are some of the reasons for which God allows us to endure hardship? Which of these have you experienced? Give examples.

11. Why is it important that a Christian trust God?

12. How should we meet trying situations when we can't see God's purpose in them?

13. In what ways is Paul's attitude a model for us?

    Optional: Share changes God has brought about in your life. How has he done this?

SUMMARY:

How is God's wisdom shown in his dealings with human beings? How can our confidence in God's wisdom be a comfort to us?

GOD'S WISDOM AND OURS

PURPOSE:
To understand God's gift of wisdom.

DISCUSSION:

1. What is the difference between an *incommunicable* and a *communicable* attribute? Name some attributes of God which fall in each category.

2. State in your own words what it means to say that man is made in God's image.

3. What does this statement mean: "God is at work in Christian believers to repair his ruined image by communicating these qualities [communicable attributes] to them afresh"?

4. What is the main thrust of the quotations about wisdom (pp. 100-101)?

5. What two steps must a person take to lay hold of the gift of wisdom? How can we do this day by day?

6. According to Packer's analogy in the "What Wisdom Is Not" section, what does having the gift of wisdom *not* mean?

7. According to Packer's analogy in the "Realism Needed" section, what does it mean for God to give us wisdom?

8. For what purpose did the author of Ecclesiastes write his sermon?

9. Read Packer's summary of the message of Ecclesiastes on pages 105-6. Then, in just a few sentences, put this message in your own words.

10. How can the admonition of Ecclesiastes help Christians today?

11. Why has God "hidden from us almost everything that we should like to know about the providential purposes which he is working out in the churches and in our own lives"?

12. According to Ecclesiastes, what is wisdom?

13. What is the effect of God's gift of wisdom?

14. What specific steps can we take to heed Packer's admonition in the chapter's final paragraph?

SUMMARY:
What is the wisdom God gives us?

THY WORD IS TRUTH

PURPOSE:

To understand the nature of God's word and consider what is an appropriate response to it.

DISCUSSION:

1. What two facts are assumed in every biblical passage?

2. For what two reasons does God speak?

3. What is the threefold character of God's *torah*? (If the meaning of any of the three terms is unclear, see examples on pp. 112-13.)

4. What does Packer mean when he says "God sends his word to us in the character of both information and invitation"? Why does God do this?

5. How does Genesis 1–3 portray God's creative word? his word of command? his word of testimony? his word of prohibition? his word of promise?

6. Why could God tell Jeremiah that Jeremiah would establish and destroy kingdoms?

7. What did God say through Isaiah about his word?

8. What is the proper response to God's word? What is an impious response? How would you characterize your own response?

9. We should believe and obey God's word primarily because it is a true word. What is *truth* in the Bible?

10. Why are God's *commands* described as true? What is the result of disobeying God's commands?

11. According to Samuel Clark, what should be some practical consequences of knowing that God's *promises* are true? What specifically can we do to reclaim the benefits of God's promises?

12. In the "Believe and Obey" section, what definition of a Christian does Packer propose? How does his extended description describe or not describe you?

SUMMARY:

How would you characterize God's word?

—*ᘓᘓᘓ*—

THE LOVE OF GOD

PURPOSE:
To try to fathom the love of God.

DISCUSSION:

1. Packer says that "to know God's love is indeed heaven on earth." What three points about God's love does Packer highlight from Romans 5:5?

2. On page 118, what criticism does Packer level at contemporary Christians? How do you react to this charge?

3. To avoid misunderstanding John's statement "God is love," what other two statements must we consider in conjunction with it? How does each one of these statements help us to understand God's love better?

4. Packer has just said, "'God is love' is *not* the complete truth about God so far as the *Bible* is concerned." What does he mean by the seemingly contradictory statement that "'God is love' *is* the complete truth about God so far as the *Christian* is concerned"? How does the love of God make a difference in *your* life day by day?

5. Packer's definition of God's love on page 123 is: *"God's love is an exercise of his goodness toward individual sinners whereby, having identified himself with their welfare, he has given his Son to be their Savior, and now brings them to know and enjoy him in a covenant relation."* What does it mean to say:
   that God's love is *an exercise of his goodness?*
   that God's love is an exercise of his goodness *toward sinners?*
   that God's love is an exercise of his goodness toward *individual sinners?*
   that God's love to sinners involves his *identifying himself with their welfare?*
   that God's love to sinners was expressed by *the gift of his Son to be their Savior?*
   that God's love to sinners reaches its objective as it *brings them to know and enjoy him in a covenant relation?*

6. Read silently the section titled "Amazing Love!" on page 127. Where in your life has God's love not had its full effect?

SUMMARY:
In your own *words*, what is the love of God? In your own *experience*, what does the love of God mean?

THE GRACE OF GOD

PURPOSE:
To understand the doctrine of grace.

DISCUSSION:

1. What two responses to the doctrine of grace are contrasted on pages 128-29?

2. What four crucial truths does the doctrine of grace presuppose?

3. In discussing these four truths, how does Packer characterize the modern pagan's view of his own morals? How does Packer characterize the modern pagan's view of God? How does such a concept of God rule out a doctrine of grace?

4. Why do some people find the doctrine of grace to be so meaningful?

5. How does your "working concept" of the doctrine of grace compare with the two views we have discussed?

6. What is the relation of *grace* and *salvation*?

7. What is *justification*? How is grace related to it?

8. What is the *plan of salvation*? How is grace related to it?

9. What is the *preservation of the saints*? How is grace related to it?

10. What does this statement mean: "In the New Testament doctrine is grace, and ethics is gratitude"? How have you experienced this in your own life?

11. Why do you think Packer says, "Those who suppose that the doctrine of God's grace tends to encourage moral laxity . . . do not know what they are talking about" (p. 136)?

    Optional: Sing one or all of the hymns quoted in this chapter. Have a time of worship, confessing your unworthiness and praising God for his grace.

SUMMARY:
What is the grace of God? How can a person *experience* it?

GOD THE JUDGE

PURPOSE:
To perceive the necessity of God's judgment—and rejoice in it.

DISCUSSION:

1. Mention a few instances in Scripture where God is referred to as Judge; where God acts as Judge; where we are taught that God is Judge.

2. What four ideas are involved in God's being a judge? Why is God able to fulfill each of these judicial functions?

3. What is *retribution*? Why does Packer say that it is "the inescapable moral law of creation"?

4. On page 143 Packer argues that God's commitment to judge people is the final proof of his moral perfection. What is Packer's argument?

5. On pages 143-44, what does Packer say is the main thrust of the reality of divine judgment?

6. What is the relation of Jesus Christ to God's judgment?

7. What is "the significance of works in the last judgment" (p. 145)?

8. Answer Packer's question: "How do free forgiveness and justification by faith square with judgment according to works?"

9. What does 1 Corinthians 3:12-15 teach Christians? How should our awareness of this affect our day-to-day living?

10. How will our *knowledge* about God affect his judgment of us?

11. What should our fear of judgment cause us to do? How will doing this affect our anticipation of the final judgment?

    Optional: Read aloud the nine Bible passages listed on p. 144. What is the main point of these passages?

SUMMARY:
Why should we rejoice in the fact that God is a judge?

THE WRATH OF GOD

PURPOSE:
To understand the nature of God's wrath.

DISCUSSION:

1. What do you think of when you hear the word *wrath*? What does the word mean? Is the Bible inhibited in speaking about God's wrath?

2. Why does the Bible speak of God *anthropomorphically*? What pitfall can this lead us into regarding God's wrath?

3. What two biblical considerations meet the charge that God's wrath is cruel?

4. What Bible passages does Packer use to support his contention that "before hell is an experience inflicted by God, it is a state for which a person himself opts"?

5. How does Packer describe *Gehenna*? How should our awareness of what it means to be separated from God affect our attitude toward non-Christians? our behavior toward them?

6. According to Romans, what is God's wrath?

7. In what ways is the constant, universal disclosure of God's wrath made?

8. How can a person be delivered from God's wrath?

9. What are some important truths that we shall never understand if we do not face the truth concerning God's wrath?

10. According to A. W. Pink, why should we meditate frequently on God's wrath?

11. How do you meet the test of "readiness . . . to meditate upon the wrath of God"?

    Optional: Read some or all of the Bible passages cited on page 149. What impression are you left with? What images are used to describe God's wrath?

SUMMARY:
What is God's wrath? What should our awareness of it motivate us to do?

GOODNESS AND SEVERITY

PURPOSE:

To learn to relate God's goodness to God's severity.

DISCUSSION:

1. Why is *and* the crucial word in Romans 11:22?

2. Why have people become so muddled in their thinking about God?

3. What is the origin of "the habit of disassociating the thought of God's goodness from that of his severity"? What effect does this habit have on Christianity? Why?

4. Why does "the Santa Claus theology [carry] within itself the seeds of its own collapse"?

5. What attributes together make up God's *goodness*?

6. Which attribute did God especially stress to Moses?

7. On page 162, what does this statement mean: "Generosity is, so to speak, the focal point of God's moral perfection"?

8. Also on page 162, what does this statement mean: "God is good to all in some ways and to some in all ways"?

9. What is the point of Psalm 145?

10. What stand out to you as the main blessings God has given you?

11. For what four examples of deliverance does the writer of Psalm 107 praise God (p. 163)?

12. What is God's severity? What does this statement mean: "Behind every display of divine goodness stands a threat of severity in judgment if that goodness is scorned"?

13. What does the entire Bible stress about the nature of God's severity?

14. What three lessons does Packer draw from his consideration of the goodness and severity of God? How can we apply each one?

    Optional: Conclude with a time of thanksgiving and praise to God.

SUMMARY:

What is the relation between God's goodness and God's severity?

THE JEALOUS GOD

PURPOSE:
To understand the nature of divine jealousy.

DISCUSSION:

1. How do we know that God is jealous? When in Israel's history did God make this especially clear?

2. How should our awareness of the Bible's use of anthropomorphisms affect our understanding of God's jealousy?

3. On page 170, what two kinds of jealousy does Packer distinguish? Why is the second kind a positive virtue?

4. How is God's jealousy an aspect of his covenant love?

5. What does God demand from those he has loved and redeemed?

6. What is the goal of God's covenant love?

7. What is God's threefold objective for this world? Why does Packer say that "it is for the securing of this end, ultimately, that he is jealous"?

8. What did God's jealousy for Israel lead him to do?

9. What are two practical consequences of God's jealousy for those who profess to be the Lord's people?

10. What is zeal? Why should jealousy for God produce it? What does the Bible say about zeal?

11. Read aloud the second full paragraph on page 174. How do you personally respond to these questions?

12. What did God say to the church at Laodicea? Would he say that to our (your) church?

    Optional: Read the verses listed near the bottom of page 168. What do they tell us about God's jealousy?

SUMMARY:
What do we mean when we say that God is jealous? What implications does this have for our personal behavior? our corporate behavior?

Optional review: What stand out to you as the main things you have learned about God's attributes in studies 7-17?

THE HEART OF THE GOSPEL

PURPOSE:

To recognize the heart of the gospel.

DISCUSSION:

1. How is biblical religion different from pagan religion? In what way is it the same?

2. What is propitiation?

3. How does propitiation relate to God's rationale for justifying sinners? to the rationale of the Incarnation? to Jesus' heavenly ministry? to John's definition of the love of God?

4. What is the difference between propitiation and expiation?

5. What is C. H. Dodd's interpretation of the "propitiation word group in the New Testament" (p. 182)? What is Packer's response?

6. In the section called "God's Anger," how does Packer characterize the wrath which was propitiated at Calvary?

7. In the next section, what three facts about propitiation does Packer state? For what reasons is each fact important?

8. What is the fundamental problem the gospel solves? How does having this central problem solved in your own life affect areas outside the center? (Be specific.)

9. How does seeing the truth of propitiation help us to understand the driving force in the life of Jesus? the destiny of those who reject God? God's gift of peace? the dimensions of God's love? the meaning of God's glory?

   Optional: What important Old Testament rituals were related to the idea of propitiation? Using a concordance or Bible dictionary, investigate each of these practices.

SUMMARY:

What is the heart of the gospel? As Packer asks, "Has the word *propitiation* any place in your Christianity?"

SONS OF GOD

PURPOSE:
To grasp the tremendous significance of adoption.

DISCUSSION:

1. Is God the Father of all people? What sort of sonship can a human being experience?

2. In what phrase does Packer sum up the whole of New Testament teaching? the whole of New Testament religion?

3. Packer says, "The revelation to the believer that God is his Father is in a sense the climax of the Bible." How does God's revelation of himself in the Old Testament compare with the New Testament revelation?

4. How does Packer refute the statement that the fatherhood of God "can mean nothing to those whose human father was inadequate"?

5. How has God made the meaning of his fatherhood clear? What are four essential elements of it (p. 204)?

6. What does Packer mean when he says that adoption is "the highest privilege that the gospel offers"?

7. Packer says that the entire Christian life has to be understood in terms of adoption. From the Sermon on the Mount, what three things does adoption serve as the basis for? How does it provide this basis?

8. Why is the phrase *adoption through propitiation*, which Packer uses on page 214, such a rich summary of the gospel?

9. How does our adoption show us the greatness of God's grace? the glory of the Christian hope? the key to understanding the ministry of the Holy Spirit? the meaning and motive of "gospel holiness"? the solution to the problem of assurance?

10. Think through (or write out) a yes or no answer to each of the questions listed at the end of the chapter. What impressions are you left with about your own understanding of adoption and your relation to your heavenly Father?

SUMMARY:
What is adoption? Why is it important?

—∽∾∾—

THOU OUR GUIDE

PURPOSE:

To learn how God guides Christians.

DISCUSSION:

1. Why is guidance a chronic problem to many Christians? Do you feel anxious about knowing God's will?

2. List the two foundation facts upon which our confidence in divine guidance rests.

3. What are some examples of divine guidance in the Bible? What are some biblical promises that God will guide?

4. What other "lines of biblical truth" confirm that God will guide (pp. 232-33)?

5. What is the basic mistake Christians make about guidance? What is the root of this mistake?

6. How does God guide his people?

7. What is God's work in "vocational" choices? What mistakes can quench the Spirit as he undertakes this work? What specific steps can we take to make sure we avoid each of these pitfalls?

8. If we step out in faith and trouble comes, how should we react? What are the main examples Packer cites on pages 239-41 to demonstrate that those who are following God may experience hardship?

9. If we take the wrong way, is the damage irrevocable? Why can we be sure it is not?

10. On pages 241-42, what essential truth about God's guidance does Packer stress? How is this a comfort to you personally?

    Optional: What are the two distinctive features of "vocational choices"? How does Hannah Whitall Smith ridicule the habit of regarding every choice as "vocational"?

SUMMARY:

How does God guide? How will knowing this affect your life?

~*~

THESE INWARD TRIALS

PURPOSE:

To recognize the harm a certain type of evangelical ministry causes.

DISCUSSION:

1. In this chapter Packer is criticizing a certain type of evangelical ministry. Why is this ministry cruel? What makes it an evangelical ministry? What, then, is wrong with it?

2. According to the "Misapplied Doctrines" section, what does this ministry stress about the difference becoming a Christian makes in a person's life? Even if these things are true, what is wrong with this emphasis?

3. What does this statement mean: "In order to appeal compellingly to human wistfulness, the type of ministry we are examining allows itself to promise . . . more than God has undertaken to perform in this world"?

4. What effect does this promise produce?

5. Why is there usually a difference between the experience of a very young Christian and of an older one?

6. What is your spiritual age? How does Packer help you understand your current situation?

7. What remedy does the ministry discussed here propose for the struggles in the Christian life?

8. When is this remedy the right one? When is it disastrous? Why?

9. At the beginning of the "Losing Sight of Grace" section, Packer levels several criticisms. What are they?

10. What is grace? What is its purpose? How does God accomplish this purpose?

11. Packer says the main curse of this kind of teaching is unreality. What reality does John Newton's hymn describe?

12. Where have you encountered the teaching Packer is opposing?

SUMMARY:

What is the primary error of the ministry Packer is criticizing?

THE ADEQUACY OF GOD

PURPOSE:

To rejoice in God's adequacy.

DISCUSSION:

(Do not spend much time on the first five questions.)

1. In what ways can Romans, "the high peak of Scripture," be read?

2. Why do some Christians have more appreciation for this book than other Christians do?

3. Why did Paul write Romans 8, "the high peak of Romans"?

4. What is the structure of Romans 8?

5. Why does Paul ask his readers in verse 31, "What, then, shall we say in response to this?"

Paul's answer to the question in verse 31 is focused in four further questions.

6. The first question is, "If God is for us, who can be against us?" What thought does this express? What does it mean to speak of "the adequacy of God as our sovereign protector"? of "the decisiveness of his covenant commitment to us"? What does the phrase *God is for us* mean to you?

7. The second question is, "He who did not spare his own Son, but gave him up for us all—how will he not also, along with him, graciously give us all things?" What thought does this express? What does it mean to speak of "the adequacy of God as our sovereign benefactor"? of "the decisiveness of his redeeming work for us"? What implications does God's claim on us have for our lifestyle?

8. The third question is, "Who will bring any charge against those whom God has chosen? It is God who justifies. Who is he that condemns?" What thought does this express? What does it mean to speak of "the adequacy of God as our sovereign champion"? of "the decisiveness of his justifying verdict upon us"? How should these truths affect us?

9. The fourth question is, "Who shall separate us from the love of Christ?" What thought does this express? What does it mean to speak of God's adequacy "as our sovereign keeper"? of "the decisiveness of divine love in settling our destiny"? To what fears in your life does this speak?

10. How has our study of knowing God brought us "to the very heart of biblical religion"?

11. How will what we have seen affect your priorities?

SUMMARY:

In describing God's adequacy, Packer uses four terms to describe God's wonderful, sovereign work in a believer's life. What are they? For which of these roles do you most rejoice?